ANIMAL PORTRAITS
ANDY ROUSE

ANIMAL PORTRAITS
ANDY ROUSE

BARNES
& NOBLE
NEW YORK

To all the conservation workers worldwide who strive tirelessly to protect our precious wildlife – you make a real difference to many lives within this book and your efforts are never in vain.

This 2007 edition published by Barnes & Noble, Inc.,
by arrangement with David & Charles, an F+W
Publications Inc. company.

ISBN-13: 978-1-4351-0420-4
ISBN-10: 1-4351-0420-X

Printed and bound in China

10 9 8 7 6 5 4 3 2 1

introduction

I love animals, in fact they are my life. The instant an animal makes a connection with me by directly looking into my lens I get a real adrenaline rush. That animal has made a conscious decision to share a moment of its life with me. It is all too often a fleeting relationship, but it is the fix that I live for as a professional wildlife photographer.

People say that you can tell a lot about someone within 15 seconds of meeting them. Well, the same is true of animals. A look is all that is needed to convey a sense of friendliness, fear, inquisitiveness or aggression. Learning to understand the look and its meaning is the skill of the wildlife photographer and amateur naturalist alike. Every living thing that I photograph has a distinct personality – the challenge for me is to capture it. Chimpanzees, for example, are always wary yet inquisitive; the land crabs of Ascension Island are feisty little chaps always ready to nip a toe if chance permits; and grizzly bears always let me know who the boss is. What makes animals fascinating is learning to decipher how they work, why they do what they do, and that, in fact, in many ways they are just like us: doing what they can to survive and raise their offspring in the best possible way.

The connection an animal makes when it looks directly down the barrel of your lens is a personal one – a split second shared between the subject and the person behind the camera. But, actually this is not the only reason photographers strive long and hard to get the perfect picture, sometimes under very unpleasant conditions and occasionally at considerable personal risk. It is first and foremost to show others just how amazing wildlife is and to foster a sense of concern for it and the habitats in which wildlife exists. Respect for nature can only be achieved through knowledge and experience, so by sharing my encounters with you in this book, I hope you will join me in appreciating the incredible natural world we live in; not only the weird and the wonderful creatures that very few of us will ever be privileged to see, but also those closer to our everyday lives such as our pets, farm animals and those in captive collections around the world.

Animal Portraits is my personally chosen selection of images from the thousands I have accumulated over the past ten years – a showcase for that fleeting moment of connection between the animal, bird, reptile, or whatever it may be, and me. It is impossible to resist seeing human-like expressions in many of the pictures – some cute and cuddly, some fearsome and dangerous, some puzzling. But whether or not it is possible to interpret their emotions in this way, direct eye contact certainly gives you the feeling that you are connecting with the mind of the animal, and all the images share this eye-to-eye relationship between the animal and you, the observer.

So come, live the life through my lens and meet our wonderful fellow inhabitants of the world.

Male Lion, Africa

Blue tit, UK

Grizzly bear, Alaska

Elephant seal, Antarctica

Arctic wolf, Canada

Grevy's zebra, East Africa

Mountain lion, USA

Wild dog, South Africa

Giraffe, South Africa

Asian elephant, Sri Lanka

Grizzly bear, Alaska

Free-range piglets, UK

Wild dog pack, South Africa

Verreaux's sifaka, Madagascar

African leopard, South Africa

Grey bamboo lemur, Madagascar

Grey seal, UK

Japanese macaque, Japan

Polar bear and cub, Canada

Chimpanzees, Zambia

African white-backed vulture, East Africa

Red grouse, UK

Hedgehog, UK

Waterbuck, South Africa

Greater kudu, South Africa

Bottlenosed dolphin, Caribbean

Lappet-faced vulture, East Africa

Hooded cobra, Sri Lanka

Mugger or marsh crocodile, Sri Lanka

Bottlenosed dolphin, Caribbean

Common brown lemur, Madagascar

Two-toed sloth, USA

Asian elephant, Sri Lanka

Cape buffalo, South Africa

Leopard, East Africa

Brown bear, Europe

Giant panda, China

Grey wolf, USA

Gannet, UK

Bengal tiger, USA

African lion, East Africa

Roan antelope, South Africa

Red fox cub, UK

Wild boar, UK

Badger, UK

Lowland gorilla, UK

Red ruffed lemur, UK

Northern lynx, USA

Cheetah cub, East Africa

Mute swan, UK

Hippopotamus, South Africa

Cape buffalo, East Africa

Scottish wildcat, UK

Spotted hyena pup, South Africa

Cheetah, South Africa

Japanese macaque, Japan

Highland cow, UK

Weasel lepilemur, Madagascar

Coati mundi, Brazil

Orangutan, Borneo

Red deer, UK

Spectacled caiman, South America

African lion, East Africa

Berkshire piglet, UK

Red fox cub, UK

White rhinoceros calf, South Africa

Elephant calf, East Africa

Roe deer fawn, UK

Lamb, UK

Red-legged partridge, UK

Puffin, UK

Spotted hyena, East Africa

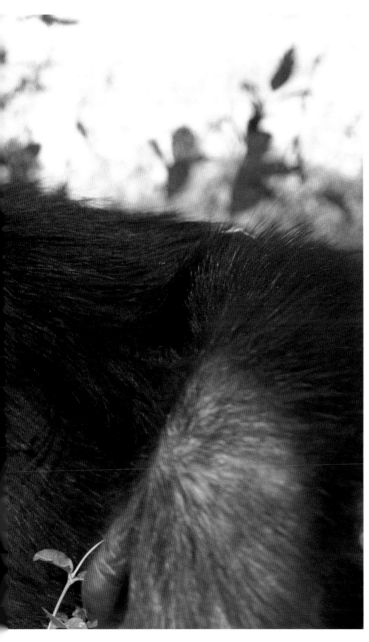

Chimpanzee, Zambia

Roe deer young, UK

Badger, UK

Meerkat, UK

Giant otter, South America

Farmyard goat, UK

Cow, UK

Orangutan youngster, Borneo

Indri lemur, Madagascar

Red squirrel, UK

Rabbit young, UK

Black-browed albatross, Falkland Islands

Rock hyrax or dassie, East Africa

Leopard cat, Thailand

African elephant herd, East Africa

Free-range piglet, UK

Devon longwool lamb, UK

Savannah baboons, Botswana

Ring-tailed lemur with baby, Madagascar

Grey seal, UK

Chinese goosling, UK

Hippopotamus, East Africa

Grizzly bear, Alaska

Orangutan youngsters, Borneo

Lambs, UK

European otter, UK

Scottish wildcat kitten, UK

Long-eared owl, UK

Indri lemur, Madagascar

Red panda, UK

Lion cub, East Africa

Elephant young and mother, UK

Masai giraffe calf, East Africa

Elderly donkey, UK

Berkshire pig, UK

Hippopotamus, South Africa

Grizzly bears, Alaska

Barn owlets, UK

Barn owl, UK

Sika deer, UK

Polar bear cub, Arctic

Grizzly bear, USA

Ewe with lamb, UK

Ring-tailed lemur, Madagascar

Rabbit, UK

Red squirrel, UK

Chimpanzee, Zambia

Black panther, USA

White rhino, UK

Little owl, UK

Tawny owl, UK

African lion cub, East Africa

Lamb, UK

Cheetah, South Africa

Masai giraffe calf, East Africa

Arctic fox, Canada

Water vole, UK

Striated caracara, Falkland Islands

Berkshire piglets, UK

Topi, East Africa

Feral goat, UK

Elephant seal bull, Falkland Islands

Cape teal, UK

Black and white ruffed lemur, Madagascar

Silvery grebe, Falkland Islands

Leopard, South Africa

Red deer, UK

Orangutan youngster, Borneo

Tawny owlets, UK

Lion cubs, East Africa

Red deer, UK

Waterbuck, East Africa

Young great grey owl, Finland

Magellanic oystercatcher, Falkland Islands

Mountain zebra foal, South Africa

Orangutan mother and young, Kalimantan

Pine marten, UK

Scottish wildcat, UK

Golden jackal, India

Grey seal pup, UK

Grizzly bear, USA

African white-faced scops owl, UK

Bengal tiger cub, USA

Changeable hawk eagle, Sri Lanka

Waxwing, Europe

Scottish wildcat kitten, UK

Leopard seal, Antarctica

Southern giraffe, South Africa

Common pheasant, UK

King cormorant, Falkland Islands

Lion cub, East Africa

Black panther, USA

Black labrador puppy, UK

Japanese macaque youngster, Japan

European kingfisher, UK

Grey mouse lemur, Madagascar

Brown hare, UK

King penguin, Falkland Islands

Stellar sea eagle, Japan

Mountain lion kitten, USA

Klipspringer, South Africa

Lambs, UK

Striated caracara, Falkland Islands

Cheetah, East Africa

Grizzly bear, Alaska

Roe deer, UK

Eastern diamondback rattlesnake, USA

Spectacled caiman, South America

Cheetah, South Africa

Ocelot, South America

Stoat, UK

Great spotted woodpecker, UK

Lion cub, East Africa

Rockhopper penguin, Falkland Islands

Lowland gorilla, UK

European otter, UK

Red-throated diver, Finland

Grizzly bear, Alaska

Cheetah with cub, East Africa

Oystercatcher, UK

Roe deer, UK

Water vole, UK

Jaguar, South America

Male lion, East Africa

European bison, Poland

Polar bear, Canada

Jaguar, South America

Spectacled caiman, South America

Grizzly bear, Alaska

Black-browed albatross chick, Falkland Islands

Brazilian tapir, South America

Toco toucan, South America

Clouded leopard kitten, UK

Southern elephant seal, Falkland Islands

Lion, East Africa

Ring-tailed lemurs, Madagascar

Asian leopard, Sri Lanka

Panther chameleon, Madagascar

King penguin, Falkland Islands

Yellow-billed stork, South Africa

Kingfisher, UK

Land monitor, Sri Lanka

Crested tit, Europe

Young ring-tailed lemur, Madagascar

Gentoo penguin, Falkland Islands

Gannets in colony, UK

Chimpanzee, Zambia

Brown bear, Europe

Arctic wolf, Canada

Mountain lion, USA

Great grey owl, UK

Indri baby, Madagascar

Mountain lion kitten, USA

Grey wolf pups, USA

Cheetah, South Africa

Tawny owl, UK

Black bear, Canada

Siberian tiger, UK

Grizzly bear, Alaska

Puffin, UK

Snowy owl, UK

Ring-tailed lemur, Madagascar

Grey wolf, Europe

Arctic wolf, Canada

Black panther, USA

Rockhopper penguin, Falkland Islands

Harp seal pup, Canada

Black rhino, South Africa

Black-browed albatross, Falkland Islands

Spectacled caiman, South America

Green-winged macaws, South America

Lowland gorilla, UK

Orangutan, Borneo

Bald eagle, UK

Acknowledgments

I would like to thank Tracey Rich for tolerating my artistic moments! I would also like to thank the following people for help in producing this book; PVV for inspiration, Howard and all at Warehouse Express, Andrew and all at ACTPIX and all of our guides who are the unsung heroes of this book. I would also like to thank Neil Baber from David & Charles who had the foresight to see the potential for the book and the determination to see it published.

Some of the animals in the book were photographed under controlled conditions. At no time was any cruelty or unethical behaviour involved, apart from bribery with the odd banana …

Andy Rouse

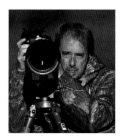

About the Photographer

Andy Rouse is one of the world's top wildlife photographers, capturing some of the most exciting and evocative photographic images seen today. His reputation is built on exciting and novel images, often conveying the experience of being up close and personal with some of the most exotic and potentially dangerous animals in the world.

His outstanding image collection covers wildlife from the frozen wastes of the Arctic and Antarctic to the stifling heat and humidity of rainforests and the scorching sun of the African plains. Passionate about the message that his images convey, he would like his work to contribute to a general appreciation of the world's animal population and stimulate people to act on their behalf. To this end, he has presented television programmes and gives talks and lectures around the world as well as writing books and articles for print and online magazines. He greatly enjoys sharing his wildlife and photographic experiences with others and frequently escorts photographic expeditions to far-flung corners of the globe.

To view the image collection or purchase a signed copy of *Animal Portraits* visit www.andyrouse.co.uk